EXETER
Characters & Personalities

*People connected with the City of Exeter
over two thousand years*

Peter D Thomas

All Rights Reserved

Printed in Great Britain

Copyright c Peter D Thomas 2009-05-14

ISBN   978-09516820-1-2
EAN   9780951682012

British Library Cataloguing in Publication Data
A catalogue record for this book is available from the British Library

EXETER CHARACTERS & PERSONALITIES
Concept, design and production
Peter D Thomas

Published by
THOMAS CASTLE
5 Abbey Road, Exeter, Devon EX4 7BG

ACKNOWLEDGEMENTS

The Author wishes to express his sincere thanks to
Mrs Margaret Smith
for her help with this publication

To
The West Country Studies Library, Devon Library Service, The Toronta Public Library,
The Castle Tea Room Maine USA,The Devon and Exeter Institution, Mrs S Hewitt, Mr Hardbottle Reed.
Mrs Sandy Adams, Mr Peter Ashmore, Mr Adrian Board, Mr John J Blackmore (Late), Mrs Pat Baker,
Mr Eric Cleave (Late)Mr George Cornish (Late),Mrs Janet Crocker ,Mrs Diane Dean,
Mr Peter Edwards, Mr B Estill (Late) Mr Nicholas Hake, Mrs Jean Levers,
Mrs Louise Phillips, Mr Shane Phillips, Mrs Elizabeth Rusbridge (Late), Mrs Margaret Smith,
Mr Christopher Stevens, Mrs Lorna Till.

DEDICATION

This book is dedicated to all the Exeter people
who supported The Exeter Historical Pageants
and helped to raise the profile of Exeter's history and heritage.

Illustrations
Some texts are illustrated with photographs by Peter Thomas of individuals who re-enacted historical
characters during The City of Exeter Pageants and costume events from 1991 to 1997

Entry of William Orange into Exeter, 5th November 1688

EXETER
Characters & Personalities
Bringing two thousand years of Exeter's people and events back to life

Early in the 1990s I was watching a single individual dressed in historical costume busking in the Cathedral Close. He attracted considerable interest. At the time I was the Tourism Promotion Officer for Exeter and running the Exeter Guided Tour service. At the next meeting with my Redcoat Guides I asked whether a few of them would consider wearing historical costume in the Cathedral Close during a lunch-time to promote the tour service. I had a rapid response and a couple of days later a few of them appeared in the Close. The reaction was instant as visitors crowded around them and cameras clicked. This small experiment started the biggest historical pageant ever to be staged in Exeter. Guides were to appear on a regular basis during the summer months handing out tour leaflets and dressed as characters from Exeter's past and local retailers greatly appreciated how visitors were drawn into the Cathedral Yard. The success led me to approach the Manager of the Royal Clarence Hotel with an idea to create an actual event. The following summer numerous guides volunteered to help and a stage, linked with a catwalk from the hotel, allowed the first period costume event to take place and attracted hundreds of people. I introduced each historical character, telling of their links with Exeter and describing their period costume. The success was repeated the following year and it was evident that if the city needed an event to raise its historical and heritage profile this was it. People loved the costumes and were fascinated by tales from the past; the guides played to the audience and the retailers were delighted with the response. The challenge was now to raise the event to a much higher level. Undertaking a great deal of research I discovered that at the turn of the 20th century Exeter had staged large historical pageants and that perhaps this could be done again. I put together a major tourism event designed to create a mid summer attraction of considerable size and duly presented it to my employer Exeter City Council. The previous event had already received plenty of publicity and at this time we were laying the foundations for tourism development in Exeter. The concept was duly passed and the task of creating the event took off. The Exeter Historical Pageant was to be the largest procession of its type to be undertaken since the turn of the century and with its launch in the press the people of Exeter embraced the idea in their hundreds and the stage was set for a major event. The concept was that the city should present 2000 years of its history and it would take place in mid season to attract as many visitors as possible. The pageant had been presented to the business community and local retailers realised the obvious benefits it would bring. A working relationship with the Express & Echo and other media raised the profile enormously. The Pageant was to be a huge historical procession and based on a previous event in 1995 in the Cathedral yard. It had presented twenty seven characters from Exeter's history that had attracted hundreds of people. The event for 1996 was going to be far larger in scale and involved the total closure of the city centre. Nearly seventy characters, all dressed in accurate period costume and supported by musicians and re-enactment groups processed through the main streets of Exeter streets supported by the Mayor and Dignitaries arriving at the Cathedral Close where the public could meet the characters, talk with them and have their photos taken. The event proved a massive success with thousands of people arriving in the city following the pre- publicity. The impact on the community lasted for weeks and there was huge excitement that Exeter was finally fully embracing its history, heritage and tourism potential.

The success was built on for 1997 with hundreds of characters, re-enactment groups, musicians and a massive staged fight in High Street, commemorating the Perkin Warbeck Rebellion. Exeter's Civic Regalia and the Sheriff's coach also played a role. It was estimated that around twenty thousand people filled the streets of Exeter. However the afternoon finale was a staged event in the Cathedral Close. To continue the event well into the afternoon I had instigated the building of a stage with a massive painted back drop of old Exeter that was erected outside the West Front of the Cathedral, after permission was granted by The Dean and Chapter. A long catwalk led from the stage out into the Cathedral Yard and right into the audience. The City Storyteller (myself) introduced the characters, described personalities, clothes and connections with Exeter. Each character processed to appropriate period music. Supported by Roman Legions, Celtic tribes, Elizabethan dancers and others the event electrified the audience for over two hours. It was estimated that around 6-8000 people watched the event in Cathedral Yard The event incorporating nearly five hundred volunteers in period costume had been an unprecedented success and proved that history, heritage and tourism development can easily go hand in hand to benefit the city. People were fascinated to learn of their past and the Exeter Historical Pageants were talked about for months and attracted substantial publicity.

The book Exeter's Characters and Personalities is based on many of the characters that took part in the Exeter Historical Pageants of 1995/1996/1997 and there are photos of some of the volunteers dressed as the character described. The costumes had been accurately portrayed by the skills of Mr John Clotworthy of Attic Costumes, Crediton, a specialist in theatrical costumes and a major supporter of the Pageants. It is hoped this book will give a greater insight into many of the interesting people that have been connected with Exeter through the ages.

Peter Thomas
Exeter
2009

Early Exeter Pageants

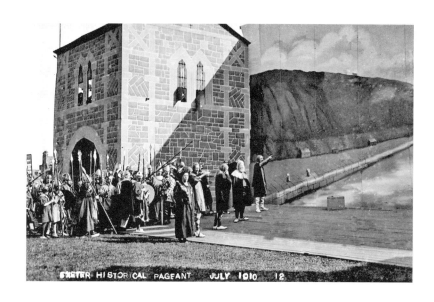

EXETER HISTORICAL PAGEANT   JULY 1910   12

Thousands came to watch, listen and learn about Exeter's colourful past at the
Exeter Hisorical Pageants and costume events from 1991 to 1997

EXETER HISTORIC CHARACTERS AND PERSONALITIES

1 Roman Legionnaire	10 King Charles I	20 Sir William Webb Follet	31 Sidney Endacott
1 Saint Sidwell	11 Princess Henrietta	20 Thomas Latimer	32 Arthur Everett
1 King Alfred the Great	11 Sir Thomas Fairfax	21 Franz Listzt	32 W H Sweet
2 King Athelstan	11 Witches	21 Queen Victoria	33 Irene and Violet Vanburgh
2 BishopLeofric	12 Richard Izacke	21 Captain Cook	33 John Shapland
2 King Edward the Confessor	12 Prince William of Orange	22 Mrs Treadwin	34 J F Widgery
3 Queen Gytha	12 Daniel Defoe	22 John Dinham	34 John Angel
3 King William the Conqueror	13 Andrew Brice	22 Charles Fowler	35 Henry Wykes
3 King Stephen	13 Dean Alured Clarke	23 Duchess of Clarence	35 Thomas Sharp
4 Bishop William Warelwast	13 John Baring	23 Mark Kennaway	36 Dr W G Hoskins
4 King John	14 Thomas Hudson	24 Reverend George Oliver	36 Herbert Read
4 Walter Gervase	14 John Patch	24 Maria Foote	37 Jacqueline Warren
5 King Edward 1	14 William Jackson	25 Willam Reginald Coutenay	37 Lady Aileen Fox
5 Walter Lechlade	15 Eleanor Coade	25 Samuel Sebastian Wesley	
5 Countess Isabella	15 Robert Trewman	25 Richard Banfill	
6 Bishop Grandisson	15 King George III	26 Charles Dickens	
6 King Edward the Black Prince	16 William Mackworth Praed	26 Sir Stafford Northcote	
6 Mayor John Attwill	16 Joanna Southcott	27 W T P Shortt	
7 King Edward IV	16 Matthew Nosworthy	27 Lloyd Parry	
7 Henry VII	17 John Graves Simcoe	28 Henry F Willey	
7 Catherine of Aragon	17 Ezekiel Abraham Ezekiel	28 Sabine Baring Gould	
8 Thomas Benet	17 Alexander Jenkins	28 Edward B Stephens	
8 Agnes Prest	18 John White abbot	29 General Redvers Buller	
8 Henry Courtenay	18 Sir Thomas Dyke Acland	29 Harry Hems	
9 Queen Elizabeth I	18 John Gendall	30 Jessie Montgomery	
9 Sir Francis Drake	19 Nicholas Prince of Russia	30 Fred Karno	
9 Sir Thomas Bodley	19 Samuel Barnes	30 Edwin Lutyens	
10 Nicholas Hilliard	19 John Stephen Bowring	31 Ethel Lega-Weekes	
10 Richard Hooker	20 Richard Ford	31 John Babbacombe Lee	

ROMAN LEGIONAIRE

In 43 AD four Roman legions invaded Britain but the penetration into the western peninsula was deferred until 55AD when Vespasian imposed a military presence on the local tribe known as the Dumnonii. The Romans built a fortress which was to form the basis of the city that was to be named Isca Dumnoniorum, today called Exeter. The legionary was an elite fighting man and with his confederates made an unbeatable force rapidly conquering the local tribe. After the Romans left around 80AD the city fell into decline and passed into a period known as the Dark Ages. Today the most notable survivor of the Roman occupation is Exeter's city wall.

SAINT SIDWELL 8th century

St Sidwell, also referred to as Saint Sidwella, was the daughter of a nobleman who lived in the 8th century. She is associated with being serene, virtuous and graceful and today is Exeter's patron saint. Sidwella was murdered by her jealous stepmother; her head being cut off with a scythe and from where her head fell to the ground water sprang out of the earth. Four nights later her figure was seen surrounded by a radiant light and carrying her head under her arm. Her body was buried at the site of today's Saint Sidwell's Church and she became Exeter's Patron Saint.

ALFRED THE GREAT 847 - 900 AD

The Anglo Saxon King Alfred was born in 847. Much of his time was taken with fighting the Vikings; however in 877 he was forced to go into hiding in the marshes of Somerset. It was here the king accepted the hospitality of a local peasant woman but infuriated her by letting her cakes burn, for which she scolded him. Exeter, a royal possession of the Saxon Kings, was re-founded by Alfred who laid out the street pattern on which Exeter is still based today. He also established a Mint and strengthened the city wall.

KING ATHELSTAN 894 - 940 AD

In 928 King Athelstan marched on Exeter and drove the ancient Britons over the River Tamar into Cornwall. Returning to Exeter Athelstan rebuilt the city wall and gates and also founded a monastery on the site of today's cathedral. The king was a regular visitor to Exeter and it is said he had his own palace in the city. His name is commemorated by a tower in Northernhay Gardens that abuts the city wall and Rougemont Castle, and is the highest point in the city.

BISHOP LEOFRIC 1016 - 1072

Exeter's first bishop, Leofric, transferred his seat from Crediton to the walled city of Exeter for greater security. King Edward the Confessor and Queen Editha enthroned him in the monastery Minster church at Exeter, which was later elevated to cathedral status.

Leofric's diocese covered the whole of Devon and Cornwall. In 1072 he founded the Cathedral Library and his eleventh century book of Anglo Saxon poetry is still found in the library. It can be viewed by the public and is called the Exeter Book.

KING EDWARD THE CONFESSOR 1004 - 1066

One of the last Saxon Kings, Edward led a holy life culminating with the founding and building of Westminster Abbey in 1065. He was made a saint in the year 1161. Edward was to marry the daughter of Earl Godwin, Editha, but the couple had a childless marriage. The King and Queen enthroned the former chaplain Leofric as the first Bishop with the founding of the cathedral in 1050. An effigy of the King and Queen is carved in stone above the High Altar in the Cathedral.

GYTHA 11th century

On the death of Earl Godwin in 1053 his Danish widow Gytha came to settle in Exeter. Her son Harold became king but was defeated by William the Conqueror at the battle of Hastings in 1066. William besieged Exeter in 1068 but his enemy Gytha escaped thanks to the help of the priest of her house church. Gytha's church, Saint Olave's still stands in Fore Street today but in an altered state.

WIILIAM THE CONQUEROR 1025 - 1087

Illegitimate William was born the grandnephew of Queen Emma of Normandy, wife of King Ethelred. He was also to become known as William the Bastard but became heir to the throne. He was ambitious, iron willed and a natural leader becoming Duke of Normandy in 1035 but he had a ruthless reputation. William the Conqueror, as he became

known, tried to claim the English throne but King Harold relented and fought losing his own life and William was crowned king of England in 1066. The City of Exeter rebelled and the enraged William marched on the city in 1068 besieging it for 18 days forcing the citizens to surrender. William ordered the building of a castle at the highest point in the city, known as Rougemont, to retain control. The original castle gatehouse, the oldest Norman gate house in England, still stands.

KING STEPHEN   1096 - 1154

Last of the Norman kings, King Stephen was born in 1097 and grew up to be handsome, good looking, easy going but weak. Stephen promised to accept the daughter of Henry 1st, Matilda, as heir to the throne but this proved to be unpopular with many English barons who supported Stephen as king. In 1135 Stephen seized the throne resulting in a civil war. Exeter Castle was besieged in 1136 when it was occupied by the Earl of Devon and his army on behalf of Matilda. The citizens refused to support the Earl and asked for help from the king. Stephen besieged the castle for three months until the wells ran dry and the garrison had consumed all their wine. They then surrendered. The Earl of Devon was exiled and the King continued his reign.

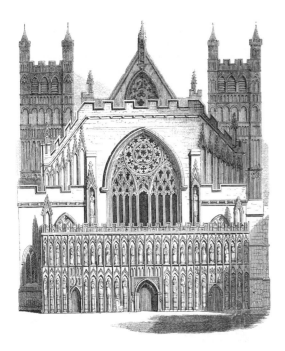

BISHOP WILLIAM WARELWAST 1107 - 1137

Bishop William Warelwast is recognised as one of Exeter's great building bishops. He was the nephew of William the Conqueror and became Exeter's third bishop in 1107. He was to take on the task of building a splendid Norman cathedral made from Beer and Salcombe Regis stone. The Cathedral was consecrated in 1133 but work continued throughout the thirteenth century. The great Norman towers still survive and have been the city's most noted feature for 900 years.

KING JOHN 1199 - 1216

The wayward King John inherited the throne from his warrior brother, Richard the Lionheart in 1199. John is remembered as a bad king and for being forced to put his seal to Magna Carta in 1215, thereby limiting the power of kings. Exeter however was grateful to King John. In 1206 he granted the citizens the right to elect a Mayor. At the time only London and Winchester had this privilege. He also showed compassion during a famine by providing food for three hundred local people for three months. John often stayed over night in the city on journeys to and from France. In 1207 he and his second wife, Queen Isabella, lodged in St Nicholas Priory of which he was very supportive. The cleanliness of the monastery suited his high standards and his liking for a good bath.

WALTER GERVASE 13th century

Walter Gervase and his father were wealthy Exeter merchants and owned waterside mills in the city. Nicholas Gervase, concerned at the loss of life with people crossing the wooden Exe Bridge during the winter months, started a scheme for its rebuilding. The money however ran out and son Walter took up the challenge. He travelled around the country persuading people of note to support the project with gifts and donations. Although Nicholas Gervase died before its completion Walter still continued. When finished the stone bridge was seven hundred feet long with seventeen fine arches. This remarkable man was elected the city's mayor in 1231 and 1239. Nearly half the ancient bridge still survives and is a National Monument.

EDWARD 1 1272 - 1307

Edward I was an outstanding king, a great soldier and statesman; also tall and athletic he was nick-named "Longshanks" He became King of England in 1272. In December 1285 Edward came to Exeter at the request of the bishop in order to attend a trial relating to the murder of the Cathedral Precentor, Walter Lechlade. He attended with Queen Eleanor and his three daughters. After the trial Edward granted an order to enclose the Cathedral Yard, the city's cemetery, by a wall incorporating seven gates. The gates would be locked at night following the ringing of a curfew bell.

WALTER LECHLADE 13th century

In 1282 Walter Lechlade was given the position of Precentor of Exeter Cathedral by Bishop Quivil. The Bishop held him in high esteem. At the time there were disagreements between the Bishop and Dean which spread to the Mayor and the town authorities. In 1283 Walter Lechlade was brutally murdered after attending matins, the first service of the day. The South Gate had been unlocked and the murderer escaped. Twenty one men were arrested including the Mayor and the Dean. At the trial two years later, attended by King Edward 1, the Mayor and the keeper of the South Gate were hanged. The Dean pleaded benefit of clergy and was confined to the Bishop's prison. One year later he had purged himself, was forgiven, and released. He was not heard of again.

ISABELLA COUNTESS OF DEVON 1237 - 1293

Isabella Countess of Devon, Albermarle and Lady of the Isle of Wight was one of the most controversial characters in the long history of Exeter and a daughter of Baldwin De Redvers. The actions of this lady caused a bitter and long lasting feud between the City of Exeter and the powerful land-owning Courtenay family, owners of Powderham Castle. In 1284 Isabella blocked the River Exe which stopped shipping coming to the Port of Exeter. She used water from the river to power a mill at Topsham. Her act lost Exeter great revenue from dues received from shipping and was to create a feud that lasted three hundred years. It resulted in the building of a new canal constructed to bypass the River Exe. It was the first Pound Lock Canal built in England.

Monument of Edward the Black Prince, in Canterbury Cathedral.

*When last I was at Exeter, the Mayor in courtesy show'd me the Castle & called it Rougemont: at which name I started, because a bard of Ireland told me once I should not live long after I saw Richmond. Richard III, Act 4, Scene 2.

BISHOP JOHN GRANDISSON
1292 - 1369

Exeter Cathedral was rebuilt in the Decorated Gothic style in the fourteenth century by Bishop John Grandisson. He devoted himself to the task and completed the work by adding the Image Screen on the West Front. His mortuary chapel was integrated into the screen and can still be seen today. The diminutive chapel was desecrated in the sixteenth century and his remains cast out. In the 1950s Bishop Grandisson's gold signet ring was found in the chapel and today can be seen in the Cathedral Library.

EDWARD THE BLACK PRINCE
1312 - 1376

Edward, The Black Prince, wore black armour in the French campaigns of the 14th century which gave him his name. He was created the first Duke of Cornwall in 1337 and Edward used Exeter as his base to tour his Duchy which included Exeter Castle. Edward's last visit to Exeter was in 1371 with his wife, the first Princess of Wales. He was taken ill during his stay and tradition says he was looked after at the house of the Mayor. The Black Prince died before his father so the crown passed to his son who became Richard III in 1377.

MAYOR JOHN ATTWILL
1440 - 1500

John Attwill, born in 1440, the son of an Exeter ship builder, was a highly regarded man being five times Mayor of Exeter. Bearing office in the reign of four kings, he was called upon to entertain two visiting Kings of England – using all his diplomatic skills to placate the first one in 1483- an angry Richard III bent on revenge. It was John Attwill who showed the King around Rougemont Castle immortalised in Shakespeare's play Richard III.

A fine stained glass window in the Thistle Hotel, Queen Street commemorates the visit of Richard III.

**CATHERINE OF ARAGON
1485 - 1536**

In 1501 Catherine of Aragon landed at Plymouth en route to marry the Prince of Wales, Prince Arthur. She stopped at Exeter for several days. She was escorted by two bishops, the Earl and Countess of Cabra, four ladies in waiting and one hundred assorted persons. Crowds gathered to see her and she proved very popular. Catherine stayed at the Deanery and was disturbed at night by the creaking weather vane of the adjacent St Mary Major Church. The offending instrument was taken down after she complained but later reinstated. Her husband Arthur died five months after their marriage. Seven years later she married Henry VIII but having no son by him the marriage was doomed. Henry defied the Pope and divorced Catherine in 1533.

EDWARD IV 1442 - 1483

Edward IV was a tall charming and handsome person and was crowned twice during the years of The Wars of the Roses. At this period the wise men of Exeter supported both sides or whoever was nearest. When Edward was about to storm the city in 1470 in pursuit of the Lancastrian sympathisers the citizens decided to placate him with a grand ceremonial welcome. The King accepted 100 gold coins from the Mayor, and was so pleased with his reception that he gave the city his sword which still rests in the Guildhall as part of the Civic Regalia.

HENRY VII 1457 - 1509

An astute businessman and the first Tudor monarch Henry VII was to rebuild the finances of England as the Royal Treasury was almost empty when he came to the throne. After his death it held several millions and his life was often threatened. In 1497 Henry came to Exeter after the city had withstood a siege under Perkin Warbeck, the Pretender to the English throne. In gratitude to the citizens of Exeter he gave a sword and Cap of Maintenance which today remain some of Exeter's greatest treasures and can be seen in the Guildhall.

THOMAS BENET   Died 1531

Thomas Benet was a school master and an early reformer having moved to Exeter in 1524. He was however to be viewed a heretic in what was then a Catholic country. Heresy carried the death penalty. Benet placed anonymous posters on the cathedral doors in October 1530 attacking the Roman Catholic doctrine. He was arrested placed in the stocks and in irons, and later brought before the Cathedral authorities He refused to retract and therefore sentenced to be burnt to death at the stake. Whilst tied at the stake a burning faggot was thrust into his face but he did not submit. The execution was carried out at Livery Dole on January 10th 1531. A memorial to Thomas Benet the martyr stands at the junction of Barnfield Road and Denmark Road.

AGNES PREST Died 1557

During the reign of Queen Mary I England returned to the Roman Catholic faith but a simple Cornish woman held on to her beliefs and paid for it with her life. Agnes Prest refused to give up her faith much to the distress of her family who tried to cure her of heresy. Finally they denounced her to Bishop Turberville of Exeter. She was arrested and put in prison for three months in Launceston but later transferred to Exeter. After still refusing to give up her faith Agnes Prest the martyr was burnt at a stake that was erected in Southernhay. She is also commemorated on the memorial in Denmark Road.

HENRY COURTENAY, MARQUIS OF EXETER, EARL OF DEVON 1496 - 1539

In 1538 the powerful Courtenay family lost all of their land, being taken by Henry VIII for an alleged conspiracy against him. Henry became suspicious and jealous of his cousin Henry Courtenay whom he executed taking all his lands for the crown. The City of Exeter was jubilant for it meant the city was free from the control of these powerful landowners. The Courtenays had blocked the River Exe to stop shipping reaching the Port of Exeter in order to obtain the Port dues. Finally in the mid 1600's the Exeter Ship Canal was constructed; by passing the river all trade was resumed with the City of Exeter.

QUEEN ELIZABETH

ELIZABETH 1   1533 - 1603
Elizabeth 1 was one of the most splendid of all British monarchs. She was surrounded by a fine court and she spoke six languages. Elizabeth became a centre of English culture and was greatly loved by the people. In 1588 she suggested the motto for Exeter *"Semper Fidelis"* (Ever Faithful) should be added to Exeter's coat of arms. It was a gesture to the city for helping to defeat the Spanish Armada. Her letter on the subject remains in the city today. She was once heard to say *"all my best men come from Devon"*

SIR FRANCIS DRAKE   1540 - 1596
Sir Francis Drake, born in Tavistock, was a sea captain, privateer, navigator, slaver and politician to Elizabeth I, and in 1580 was the first Englishman to sail around the world. He returned with a ship full of treasure for the queen who knighted him aboard the ship The Golden Hind in 1581. He became a national hero and favourite of the queen. In 1588 Drake fought the Spanish Armada in the English Channel and defeated them using a fleet of 34 ships against 130 Spanish galleons. Drake often visited Exeter and wrote a letter stating *"next to my own ship I do most love that old ship in Exon a tavern in St Martins Lane"*

SIR THOMAS BODLEY   1544 - 1613
Brilliant scholar and linguist, Sir Thomas Bodley was the founder of the present day Bodleian Reference Library at Oxford University. He was born in Exeter in 1544 and later came to the notice of Queen Elizabeth I who appointed him a Gentleman Usher to her court and then as her diplomat abroad. After serving as MP for Plymouth he returned to Oxford to devote his life to extending his library which he opened in 1603 with 2000 volumes. In 1604 he was knighted by King James I who remarked his name should have been *Godly* and not *Bodley.*

NICHOLAS HILLIARD 1547 - 1619

The son of an Exeter goldsmith Nicholas Hilliard was producing miniature paintings at the age of thirteen. He was extrovert, charming and impulsive and trained in London as a jeweller and goldsmith. At the age of twenty-three he was appointed as the painter of miniatures to Queen Elizabeth I. Nicholas Hilliard produced many fine works for the royal court with his most famous work being the Armada Jewel created in 1580. It is a miniature of the queen in an enamelled frame studded with diamonds and rubies. Today it can be seen in The Royal Victoria and Albert Museum, London.

RICHARD HOOKER 1553 – 1600

Richard Hooker, was born in Exeter in 1553 and is recognised as an outstanding theologian of his time creating the book *The Laws of Ecclesiastical Polity* published in 1594. He attended Exeter Grammar School and was later to attend Corpus Christi College Oxford. He completed five books but three further volumes were not published until the 17th century. Richard Hooker is commemorated by a fine statue that stands in the Cathedral Yard that was erected in 1907 by his descendants at a cost of one thousand guineas. His uncle was Exeter historian John Hooker.

CHARLES I *AND HENRIETTA MARIA* 1600 - 1649

Charles I, a small, fastidious and religious man, was self disciplined with scrupulous morals. He became king on 27th March 1625 and married the fifteen year old Henrietta Maria, daughter of Henry IV of France. She was a staunch Roman Catholic and was feared by her English people. Charles disagreement with Parliament led to the Civil War. In 1644 the pregnant queen was sent to Exeter for safety. She gave birth to the only royal person ever born in the city, Princess Henrietta. The queen fled for France leaving her daughter behind and she never saw Charles again. She died in France at the age of 60. King Charles came to Exeter twice during the civil war.

PRINCESS HENRIETTA 1644 - 1670

Henrietta Anne was born on 16th June 1644 in Bedford House, Exeter and christened in the Cathedral. Two years later she was smuggled out of the country to France where she joined her mother, dressed as a boy to conceal her identity. Henrietta married Philippe of Orleans, the brother of King Louis XIV. It was not a happy marriage. In 1670, at the age of twenty six and against her husband's wishes she was sent to England by Louis to negotiate the secret Treaty of Dover with her brother Charles II. One month later she returned from France became ill and died. It is said she was poisoned by her husband. Her portrait, presented to the City of Exeter by her brother, still hangs in the Guildhall.

THOMAS FAIRFAX 1612 - 1671

Sir Thomas Fairfax was for some years Commander in Chief of the Parliamentary armies in the Civil War. In 1645 Fairfax was sent by Cromwell to subdue Devon with the New Model Army. He captured Bridgwater, then Tiverton Castle and then blockaded Exeter.

In March 1646 he returned to raise the siege of Exeter signing a treaty on April 9th at Poltimore House, near Exeter, where the "Ever Faithful" city surrendered to Parliament. Later that week Fairfax and Cromwell were invited to supper by the Mayor where they were treated with great respect.

EXETER WITCHES   17th century

In the seventeenth century anyone thought to be practising witchcraft was liable to be hanged and it is said the last witch in England lived in Exeter in 1684. Three old women from Bideford, all poor, ugly and discontented were tried at the Assizes in Exeter on 18th August 1682 and found guilty. Temperance Lloyd, Susanna Edwards and Mary Trembles were all hanged. In 1684 Alice Molland was said to have used effigies and by sticking pins in them caused the bodies of three ladies to swell up. It was said she could make children walk up walls backwards. Defiant Alice stood upright in the cart as they took her to the gallows.

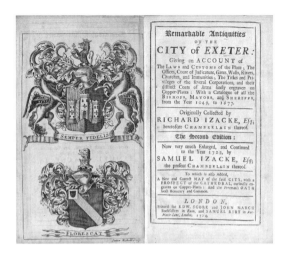

RICHARD IZACKE 1623 - 1697

Author Richard Izacke is renowned for his book *Remarkable Antiquities of the City of Exeter from 1049-1677* printed in 1677 and its production was financially supported by the City Chamber. It is one of Exeter's earliest printed books and was printed in three editions. It was first enlarged by his son Samuel Izacke in 1724 who included a map and Prospect of the Cathedral. Richard Izacke was destined to be a lawyer and entered the Inner Temple on 25th October 1653, he was also elected as Chamberlain of Exeter. In 1663 he became Town Clerk. A diligent and respected man Richard Izacke died in the Cathedral Close on 13th March 1697 at the age of 74.

PRINCE WILLIAM OF ORANGE 1650 -1702 then KING WILLIAM III 1689 -1702

Prince William of the Netherlands and his English wife Princess Mary were invited to take the English throne from Mary's father, the much feared King James II – in order to uphold the Protestant faith. William landed at Brixham with a magnificent army of fifteen thousand well disciplined men on 5th November 1688. On arrival at Exeter he established a temporary court at the Deanery. He drank the Dean's wine and sat on the Bishop's throne as both dignitaries had fled the city. William remarked *"Exeter's defences could have been flattened with baked apples"*. Nevertheless the citizens were overjoyed to see him and he drew massive support on his march to London. King James fled into exile, dropping the Great Seal of England into the Thames on his way to France. The conclusion of this bloodless "Glorious Revolution" was that William and Mary were crowned joint King and Queen of England in 1689.

DANIEL DEFOE 1659 – 1731

London born Daniel Defoe, author, journalist and secret agent was born in 1660. As an author his most well known novels are Robinson Crusoe, and Moll Flanders. While compiling a three volume travel book in 1724 he visited Exeter and was suitably impressed. He wrote *"Exeter is large, rich, beautiful, populous and was once a very strong city"* He noticed Exeter was full of gentry, good company, trade and manufacture. *"The cloth market is well worth seeing"* he said *"and next to the Brigg market in Leeds is the greatest in England, with a weekly turnover of sixty to one hundred thousand pounds.*

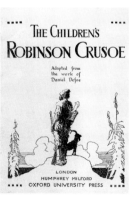

ANDREW BRICE 1690 - 1773

Andrew Brice, printer and poet, was the son of an Exeter shoemaker and born in Exeter in 1690. Although originally destined to be a minister he was apprenticed as a printer at the age of seventeen. He was for a short period of time a soldier but returned to Exeter to set up his own printing press called *"Postmaster"* or *"Loyal Mercury"*. He was frequently involved with legal problems and at one time had to appear in The House of Commons for falsely printing the proceedings of the House; he was to continue his work publishing stories and poems despite running into severe difficulties, becoming nearly bankrupt. He was particularly fond of the

theatre and came to the aid of players who were being persecuted in 1745. Although married twice none of his wives or children outlived him. Many West Country books were published by him. Andrew Brice died on November 7th 1773 and was buried in Bartholomew Yard Cemetery.

DEAN ALURED CLARKE
1696 - 1742

Dr Alured Clarke had previously been a Prebendary of Winchester Cathedral before coming to Exeter. In 1741 he was appointed Dean of Exeter and decided to found a hospital as he had done in Winchester. To create his hospital for the poor he enlisted the help of county society, and the MP for Exeter John Tuckfield gave land in Southernhay as a building site. Dean Clarke, one of Exeter's great benefactors, was to die before the completion of the hospital in 1743.

Larkbeare House

JOHN BARING 1697 - 1748

In 1717, at the age of twenty, John Baring, the son of a Lutheran pastor, emigrated from Bremen to Exeter to study the serge making industry and became a successful textile merchant. His success began the history of the oldest merchant banking company in the country. He lived in old Larkbeare House, purchased in 1727, at the bottom of Holloway Street. John Baring died at an early age in 1748 leaving two sons who became involved in business as merchants and bankers. In 1770 John Baring junior opened the Devonshire Bank at number 193 High Street adjacent to Parliament Street. He became the Exeter MP and purchased much of the parish of St Leonard's. Francis Baring went to London and became a company agent and importer connected with the wool trade. The Baring brothers became world famous millionaires. The Baring Bank they created collapsed in 1995.

THOMAS HUDSON 1701 - 1779

Born in Exeter in 1701 Thomas Hudson became a popular portrait artist. His work was admired for its faithful reproduction of the sitter. From a privileged background Hudson undertook his work under the mentorship of Jonathan Richardson, a well known contemporary artist. Paintings were only partly executed with unimportant detail undertaken by assistants. Joshua Reynolds was to become a pupil of Hudson but was a better artist than the master. Hudson, who painted George III, Chief Justice Pratt and the Duke of Marlborough, retired to Twickenham. The artist died on January 26th 1779.

JOHN PATCH Junior 1724 - 1787

John Patch junior, an eminent Exeter surgeon, was trained by his father, who was also a senior surgeon at the newly opened Royal Devon and Exeter Hospital. John proved to be a brilliant scholar and later went to Edinburgh where he married. With the death of his father in 1746 John took over his position at the hospital and became a noted surgeon and held in high esteem. He was an encyclopaedia of medical information. In 1769 he built a house next to Rougemont Castle and created a wonderful landscaped garden that incorporated the dry moat and castle slope. The house was bought by the City Council and the grounds opened to the public on 2nd April 1912. The house was transformed into a local history museum.

WILLIAM JACKSON 1730 - 1803

William Jackson, painter and musician was born in Exeter in 1803 where his grandfather made a fortune from the making of serge cloth but his father rapidly spent the family money leaving William to stand very firmly on his own two feet. He was to become a painter and a friend of the artists Gainsborough and Joshua Reynolds, but his first love was music. William became an accomplished musician, teacher and organist, taking up a position as Cathedral organist in 1777. Noted for his sacred music and instrumental pieces he created three masterpieces for London audiences. In 1882 he also wrote his biography and was often referred to as Jackson of Exeter.

ELEANOR COADE 1733 - 1821

Exeter born Eleanor Coade, the daughter of a Lyme Regis wool merchant, became famous for the production of artificial stone. The stone suited the creation of works of art being capable of showing fine detail and was particularly hard wearing. Eleanor was to keep the actual formula most secret, for its durability was its most noted asset. While in her thirties Eleanor Coade bought a factory in Lambeth London where all manner of decorative items were produced. Her works of art were to gain high recognition being purchased and displayed in prominent houses, gardens and public places. She exported her products and was patronised by royalty. The famous Regency terraces of Southernhay, Exeter are decorated with Coade Stone keystones each bearing an individual face.

ROBERT TREWMAN 1738/9 - 1802

Printer and bookseller Robert Trewman and a partner worked for the Exeter printer Andrew Brice, but were to start their own newspaper, *The Exeter Mercury* or *West Country Advertiser*. The first issue was on 2nd September 1763. Robert Trewman was to found Trewman's Flying Post and in 1781 purchased number 226 High Street, a period building. The newspaper was to be printed from the building for eighty-one years but the property was used for printing purposes for one hundred and seventy seven years. Printer and bookseller Trewman printed the book *The ancient history and description of Exeter* and a copy was presented to George III in 1789 on his visit to Exeter. Robert Trewman died at number 226 High Street in 1802 and was buried in the family tomb in Bartholomew Street Cemetery.

GEORGE III 1738 - 1820

George III and his Queen Charlotte, visited Exeter in 1789 accompanied by three of their daughters. They had fifteen children. The couple were received at the site of the old East Gate and a procession of two hundred respectable tradesmen, special constables, and Members of the Chamber processed through the city to the Deanery and a service held in the Cathedral. George's views of kingship conflicted with the constitution and he sought to rule without regard for party politics. His policies led to the American War of Independence and the loss of the colonies. In the latter years of his life he suffered from blindness and recurring bouts of madness.

WILLIAM MACKWORTH PRAED
1747 - 1833

Cornishman William Mackworth Praed, Banker and Politician, had a country seat at Bitton near Teignmouth Devon. He inherited derelict property in Exeter's High Street and set about its restoration. Praed became aware that Exeter was lacking in facilities for public entertainment and social gatherings and with the help of partners set about building an Assembly Room in the Cathedral Close. The building, dated 1769, became known as The Royal Clarence Hotel and the first "hotel" in England. However in conjunction with the Assembly Room a bank was constructed that was to form part of the side of St Martins Lane. The Exeter Bank operated until 1905. At a later date the building was integrated with The Royal Clarence Hotel.

JOANNA SOUTHCOTT
1750 – 1814

Joanna Southcott, born of humble surroundings in 1750 in Exeter, was to become a domestic servant and upholsteress. She attracted interest later in her life professing to have dreams and visions and that she was the chosen one to become the Mother of Shiloh, Prince of Peace, and prophesy forthcoming events. Joanna became a well known character and gave up her work due to having created a following and believed she would not die. She became a religious fanatic and gathered followers from across three counties. At the age of 64 she predicted she would give birth to a son and a date was given by her for the event, being October 19th. However it did not transpire but Joanna died ten days later. She produced sixty publications during her lifetime.

MATTHEW NOSWORTHY
1750 - 1831

Matthew Nosworthy, born in Widecombe in the Moor, came to Exeter at an early age. He started his own building company and responsible for giving Exeter much of its Georgian architectural character. Imposing terraced houses were built in Southernhay between 1790 and 1820 of which Dix's Field and Barnfield Crescent are noted examples. In May 1792 the building of Barnfield Crescent, was contracted to Matthew Nosworthy and consisted of twenty seven houses. The construction continued until 1806. He also built The New London Inn in the 1790s and houses in Colleton Crescent. Although devastated in WWII Exeter still retains many of Nosworthy's original buildings. Matthew Nosworthy died in 1831 at the age of eighty one.

JOHN GRAVES SIMCOE 1752-1806

John Graves Simcoe became the first Lieutenant Governor of Upper Canada in 1792. He is one of the best known Governors of any British North American colony and is remembered by Canadians as the father and founder of Ontario. Born on February 25th 1752 in the Cathedral Close Exeter, a plaque now commemorates his birthplace. His early education took place in Exeter but he continued to Eton and Oxford before joining the 35th Regiment of Foot in 1770. He fought the American War of Independence in 1775 in command of the Queen's Rangers. His last post was Colonel in Chief of British Forces in India. On the outward journey he became ill and returned to Exeter where he died at Number 12 Cathedral Close. He was buried at Wolford Chapel on the family estate near Honiton. The chapel was acquired by the Ontario Heritage Foundation in 1982.

EZEKIEL ABRAHAM EZEKIEL 1757 - 1805

The son of a Jewish silversmith and watchmaker, Ezekiel Abraham Ezekiel was born in Exeter in 1757. He was one of six children. Ezekiel was apprenticed at the age of fifteen in 1772 to goldsmith Alexander Jenkins but in 1779 produced his first engraving titled A Perspective View of Bideford. His reputation as an engraver spread, and in 1784 he advertised his business skills including copper plate, bills of exchange, book plates and trade plates. He also started to produce fine portraits of important people. Ezekiel expanded his business further

becoming one of the first opticians in the West Country, a Miniaturist, and also instrumental in the building of Exeter's first synagogue in 1763. Unmarried Ezekiel lived with his brother and two sisters at 170 Fore Street. With Ezekiel's death, at the age of 48, his brother Henry gave engravings by him to the Devon and Exeter Institution in Cathedral Close where they can still be seen today.

ALEXANDER JENKINS 1738 - 1825

Alexander Jenkins was born on the 26th May 1738 in the parish of St Mary Major, Exeter. Alexander was apprenticed as an engraver, by his father who was a joiner, and was to become intensely interested in the history and antiquity of his native city. The fruits of his labours were produced in the book *"The history and description of the City of Exeter and its environs, Ancient and Modern, Civil and Ecclesiastical "* printed in 1806. Jenkins died on 16th December 1825.

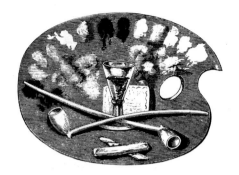

JOHN WHITE ABBOTT 1763 - 1851

The artist, John White Abbott, was born in Exeter in 1763 and became an Apothecary and surgeon in Exeter but also took a great interest in art and painting. His uncle, who also taught watercolour painting supported him, and introduced him to important people in the artistic world including Sir Joshua Reynolds. John White Abbott was a skilled draughts-man which is seen in his work. He was to exhibit at The Royal Academy from 1793 to1805 but never sold any of his paintings throughout his life. He was to inherit a substantial estate on the edge of Exeter and retired early to live the life of a country landowner. He died in 1851. Today his work is highly sought after.

THOMAS DYKE ACLAND 1787 - 1871

A statue of Thomas Dyke Acland, that now stands against the city wall in Northernhay Gardens, was originally placed centrally in the castle courtyard in

October 1861. Born in 1787 Thomas Dyke Acland of Killerton was the eldest of five brothers and was to marry in 1808 and father ten children.. A moderate Tory he was elected to Parliament on 15th October 1812 and re-elected in 1830. Due to political pressure he retired in 1831 but rejoined Parliament in 1837. Thomas was keen to maintain his estates, which had often caused him financial problems but he also supported charities.

JOHN GENDALL 1789 - 1865

Baptised 2nd January 1790 John Gendall came to Exeter as servant to James White in the Cathedral Close. White was to recognise the talent of his servant and arranged introductions for John in London. He obtained a position with Rudolph Ackermann, being involved with the lithographic process and became a fine draughtsman. As an artist he produced views of London and excelled in watercolour and drawing and worked in Hastings, Dover, Calais and Edinburgh. Between 1819 and 1827 he undertook views of country houses of which some were published in "Views of Country Seats" in 1830. John Gendall died on 1st March 1865. Illustrations by the artist showing scenes of Exeter were supplied to his friend Thomas Shapter for inclusion in his book "*The Cholera in Exeter 1832*"

PRINCE NICHOLAS OF RUSSIA 1796 - 1855

The advent of street lighting by gas in Exeter was to attract one of the city's most unusual visitors in 1817, Nicholas of Russia. So new was the idea that the prince came to see for himself what this extraordinary invention was about. He was received by Landlord Samuel Foot at *"The Hotel on the Green"*, now The Royal Clarence Hotel. Of medium build, with dark hair and beard, the Duke was poorly educated. However twelve years after his visit to Exeter he was crowned Tsar of all the Russians. Later known as The Iron Tsar, his policies resulted in England being at war with Russia.

SAMUEL BARNES 1776 - 1858

Samuel Barnes, born in 1776, was the son of an Archdeacon of Totnes and Chancellor of Exeter Cathedral. He was educated at Exeter Grammar School, the Hunterian School London and attended St Bartholomew's Hospital for two years before finally returning to Exeter. He practiced ophthalmic surgery at the Devon and Exeter Hospital from 1813 and became a skilled demonstrator of anatomy. He lived at number five Barnfield Crescent. Barnes retired in 1846 but became a member of the Honorary Consulting Staff. From 1813 to 1858 he was the secretary of the Devon and Exeter Institution in Cathedral Close where a fine bust of him by Samuel Bouverie can be seen. It was presented by subscription and exhibited at the Royal Academy. Samuel Barnes died in December 1858.

SIR JOHN BOWRING 1792 - 1872

Exeter born John Bowring was to become a student of literature and foreign languages in which he specialised. His knowledge extended to two hundred languages with the ability to speak one hundred. In 1825 he became the editor of the Westminster Review and promoted free trade and parliamentary reform through its pages. In 1835 he became a Member of Parliament and invested in the iron industry of South Wales. In 1849 he became the British Consul for Canton and supervised trade with China. In 1854 he took on the role of Governor for Hong Kong and later Commissioner to Italy in 1861. John Bowring was MP for Exeter from 1868 to 1874.

He died at the age of 80 near Exeter on 23rd November 1872. Sir John Bowring was President of the Devon and Exeter Institution in Exeter from 1860 to 1861. A bust of him was presented to the library in 1983.

RICHARD FORD   1796 - 1858

Richard Ford, nineteenth century travel writer, artist and authority on Spain was born in London in 1796 and graduated at Trinity College, Oxford. He spent four years in Spain with his sick wife later returning to England where his wife died in 1837. Ford came to live in Southernhay and bought Ford House at Heavitree in 1898 converting the gardens into a Moorish style. He was to write the definitive guide book to Spain titled *A Handbook for Travellers in Spain* that continues to be a major work on the country. Richard Ford died on 31st August 1858 of Bright's Disease and his son sold Heavitree House in 1898. In a poor state of repair the building was demolished in 1958.

SIR WILLIAM WEBB FOLLET 1798 - 1845

The English lawyer Sir William Webb Follett was born in Topsham in 1798. He was educated at Exeter Grammar School

and Trinity College Cambridge and called to the Bar in 1824 and was to have a very prestigious career. His qualities were soon evident and he was recognised for his perception, judgement and temperament. In 1834 he was appointed Solicitor General and knighted in 1835. In the same year he became an MP for Exeter until 1845 but also took on the role of Attorney General in 1844. Plagued with bad health in later life Sir William died on 28th June 1845. He is known as the greatest Advocate of the century.

THOMAS LATIMER 1803 - 1888

Bristol born Thomas Latimer was apprenticed to a printer but became a well known campaigning newspaper editor.

In 1827 he took up a post as a reporter for the Exeter News and Devon County Chronicle and attended the Exeter Assizes. He was to become an avid campaigner for penal reform and the removal of the death penalty. Latimer purchased a fine early 18th century house in Fore Street, Exeter and it was to be a printing house and distribution depot for London newspapers from 1840. Latimer and Charles Dickens struck up a friendship as young reporters and Dickens often stayed with his friend. Latimer was to fight for the common man through his newspaper The Western Times and often fought against the system. The reforming editor also revolutionised aspects of the printing industry with technological improvements leading to increased newspaper production. Latimer died on January 5th 1888

FRANZ LISZT 1811 - 1886

The great Hungarian composer and pianist Franz Liszt began his public career in 1820 at the age of nine. He was known as "The Hungarian Wonder Child". During his grand tour with a small group playing his own compositions and songs, he received rapturous applause from thousands of people across Europe. Liszt gave two performances at The Royal Clarence Hotel in August 1840. The hotel overlooking the green grass and graceful trees of the Cathedral Yard prompted him to write to his mistress *"English cathedrals are more impressive than those in France because they are not crowded round with shops and buildings"*. His best known compositions today are his Hungarian Rhapsodies.

QUEEN VICTORIA 1819 - 1901

Queen Victoria was born in 1819 and came to the throne at the age of 18. In 1840 she married Prince Albert of Saxe Coburg. The couple were devoted and had nine children and were to greatly influence Parliament. On Albert's death in 1861 Victoria fell into deep mourning and isolated herself from Parliament and the people. Concern grew for the Queen and for the country's future as she was not carrying out her duties. Finally the Prime Minister Benjamin Disraeli used his powers of persuasion and Victoria was to finally reign over one quarter of the world's surface. Victoria, Albert and young Prince Arthur visited Plymouth in 1856 but seasickness forced their return to London stopping at Exeter. The City welcomed Victoria. She accepted three bouquets of flowers but declined a bowl of fruit.

CAPTAIN JOHN COOK Circa 1820

One of Exeter's ancient traditions was escorting judges for their security to and from the Assizes at Exeter Castle. In the 19th century a group of twenty four men would be chosen from the Devon Constabulary. Called Javelin Men, as each carried a Javelin or pointed spear, their job was to protect the judges. Javelin men would first assemble with their horses at Mr John Cook's, a saddler in central High Street to have their saddle cloths put on. John Cook, referred to as Captain Cook and dressed in a scarlet hat, coloured breeches also carried a javelin and led the Javelin Men who preceded the Sheriff's coach carrying the judges. This was undertaken on entering and leaving the city. Captain Cook became a well known character to many Exeter people as he was outgoing and a self publicist.

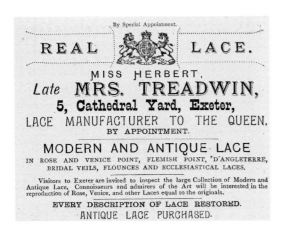

MRS TREADWIN 1820 – 1890

Charlotte Treadwin was born in 1821 and became the most important figure in the history of Honiton Lace. Her premises at No 5 Cathedral Close ran for forty years from 1867. She received her first royal warrant in 1848 which was followed by further commissions. Mrs Treadwin's work was also exhibited in the Great Exhibition in 1851 and won awards in Paris and London. A great experimenter she was to have a marked effect on this local industry.

JOHN DINHAM   1788 – 1864

John Dinham is noted as being one of Exeter's benefactors during the Victorian period and is commemorated by a statue in Northernhay Gardens. Early in his career he became bankrupt but worked to change the situation, becoming a wealthy man. He was a man of integrity and supported numerous charities and benevolent societies and was particularly interested in the education of working class children. John Dinham was to instigate the building of twenty four Free Cottages on the site of Mount Dinham having a spectacular view over the River Exe. John Dinham died in 1864 and was buried in the Lower Cemetery in Bartholomew Street, overlooked by the site at Mount Dinham.

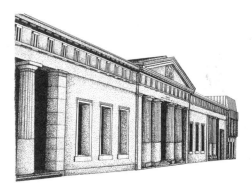

CHARLES FOWLER 1792 – 1867

Architect Charles Fowler was born in 1792 at Cullompton and specialised in designing covered markets. His most famous design was used for London's Covent Garden. His early training took place in Exeter but he was to return to design the city's Lower Market which opened in 1835. His design was the result of a competition that he entered to find the best architect for the new building. He created a substantial building of Italianate design with a massive hall and prominent towers. Much of the structure was built from large granite blocks. The market was bombed in 1942 and the remains demolished. However Charles Fowler's other masterpiece still stands. The Higher Market in Queen Street was opened in 1838 but radically changed in the 1970s for the creation of the Guildhall Shopping centre. The market's façade now forms an impressive entrance into the shopping centre.

THE DUCHESS OF CLARENCE 1818 - 1849

The name of The Duchess of Clarence has been immortalised with one of Exeter's most prominent buildings The Royal Clarence Hotel. The Duchess of Clarence was to become Queen Adelaide, wife of William IV. In 1827 she was a guest at the hotel referred to as *the hotel in the churchyard*. The hotel was to be renamed in her honour. She revisited Exeter on a number of occasions. In 1845 she returned but as The Dowager Queen Adelaide and arrived by train, a new form of transport at the time.

MARK KENNAWAY 1793 - 1875

Mark Kennaway was born into a well known Exeter family of Wine Merchants who had primarily made their wealth from the woollen cloth trade but continued into the exporting of wine. Mark Kennaway became a solicitor in Exeter and a councillor being noted for his good voice and fluency of speech. The complex of almshouses known as Wynard's in Magdalen Street had been aquired by the Kennaway family in 1789 when the properties were restored, and a family vault constructed under the chapel. Mark Kennaway created a side entrance from the street into the chapel between 1856-8 but also undertook restoration of the chapel, inserting a fine stained glass window. He also commissioned a superb full length memorial brass of George Glass Kennaway in 1869 for the chapel floor. It is now recognised as an excellent and rare example. The complex of buildings remained with the family until the 1950s when they were handed over to the Exeter Municipal Charities. Today the Almshouses and chapel have become private dwellings and a gated community. The mausoleum of the Kennaway family still remains below the chapel.

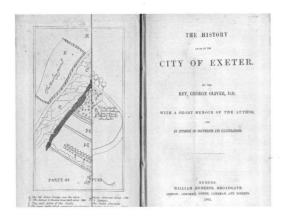

REVEREND GEORGE OLIVER 1781 - 186

Born in 1781 at Newington Butts London on 9th February George Oliver was destined to be a priest. He was educated at Sedgeley Park and Stoneyhurst becoming a teacher of Humanities. He was ordained in 1806 at Durham and appointed to The Exeter Mission at Exe Island in 1807, living in the historic St Nicholas Priory off Fore Street, Exeter. Oliver studied history and antiquities and was to be recognised as an authority on civil and ecclesiastical history in Devon and Cornwall. In 1843 he was made an Honorary Member of the Historical Society of Boston and a Doctor of Divinity by Pope Gregory in September 1844. George Oliver produced a number of literary works including *The Monasticon of the Diocese of Exeter, The lives of the Bishops of Exeter and*

A history of Exeter Cathedral and The History of the City of Exeter published in 1861. The Reverend George Oliver died after a stroke on March 23rd 1861. Following his death an advertisement stated *"It is respectfully announced that a bust (recently taken from life) of the late Dr Oliver is now prepared and casts will be ready in a few days. The likeness is most faithful and the bust will be mounted on a pedestal bearing an inscription, devices. The model may be seen and casts obtained at Mr G Smith's, Organ Builder, 10 Lansdowne Terrace, Exeter"*.

MARIA FOOTE   1798 - 1867

Maria Foote, born in 1798, was the daughter of Samuel Foote, dramatist of Plymouth. In 1810 at the age of twelve she acted in her father's theatre at Plymouth and in 1814 took part in a production at Covent Garden. Renowned as being a beautiful girl she became the mistress of Colonel Berkley, Lord Segrave and Earl Fitzharding. Maria made a number of appearances in Exeter and the public adored her. She was not however noted for her acting ability with her last stage appearance being in 1831. In the same year she married Charles Stanhope 4th Earl of Harrington becoming a countess at the age of 33. He was 51. Maria Foote died at the age of 69.

WILLIAM REGINALD COURTENAY 1807 - 1888

Born in 1807 William Reginald Courtenay was educated at Westminster College, London and Christchurch College Oxford and became a Bachelor of Law, Master of Arts and received an honorary degree in 1838. He became a Member of Parliament for South Devon from 1841-1849. In 1859 he was elevated to the title of eleventh Earl of Devon and held the office of Chancellor of the Duchy of Lancaster in 1866 and was an Honorary Colonel of the Royal First Devon Yeomanry Cavalry. He died at the age of 81 in 1888. A bronze statue was erected to him in 1880 at Bedford Circus and in the late post war period it stood at the junction with High Street and Bedford Street. Now in storage, it may be placed in Northernhay Gardens.

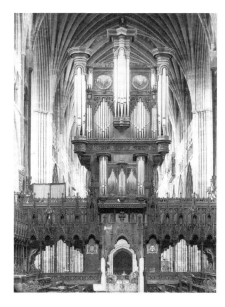

SAMUEL SEBASTIAN WESLEY 1810 - 1876

The magnificent organ in Exeter Cathedral, built by John Loosemore in 1660 has been played by some outstanding organists. One of the most famous was London-born, Samuel Sebastian Wesley, who became the Cathedral Organist at the age of 25 in 1835. He had published a great deal of church music. Samuel improved the standard of the choir and the musical standards of the Cathedral. However he came into conflict with the church authorities and eventually took a post as organist at Leeds. He always had a deep affection for Exeter and on his death his body was brought back to the city to be buried with his baby daughter.

RICHARD BANFILL Circa 1810 - 1880

The ancient title of Wharfinger was given to the person responsible for the management of shipping and the affairs of the Port of Exeter. In 1823 Richard Banfill started work as a clerk on Exeter's Quay but later became its Wharfinger. His career was to span 60 years and during his lifetime he saw ships tied three deep and up to thirty vessels lining the quay. He witnessed the decline of the Port with the advent of the railway from the 1840s. The Wharfinger's office bearing the city coat of arms still exists on the quay but the title of wharfinger is no longer used.

CHARLES DICKENS 1812 - 1870

The famous Victorian novelist Charles Dickens was born in Portsmouth in 1812 and as a young man became a journalist. He never forgot the difficulties experienced in his early years and became a great social campaigner. Charles Dickens often visited his friend and fellow journalist Thomas Latimer at his house in Fore Street, Exeter. Dickens was to be inspired whilst in Exeter by characters seen in the Turks Head pub next to the Guildhall. One of his book characters, the Fat Boy, was based on a boy seen there who is depicted in The Pickwick Papers.

As a prolific author Dickens produced some of the finest novels ever written including Oliver Twist, A Christmas Carol, David Copperfield, Great Expectations, Bleak House and Little Dorit. Charles Dickens died of a stroke in 1870 at the age of 58 leaving ten children.

SIR STAFFORD NORTHCOTE 1818 - 1887

The distinguished statesman and Baron of Northcote, Pynes, was born in 1818 and educated at Eton and Oxford. He became private Secretary to the Prime Minister Mr Gladstone, Financial Secretary to the Treasury, President of the Board of Trade and Secretary of State for India for conservative administration. Stafford Northcote also represented Dudley, Stamford and latterly North Devon. A statue was erected to him on October 19th 1887 in Northernhay Gardens, where it can still be seen today. The sculpture showing him dressed as a peer of the realm is of white marble and the work of Joseph E Boem. An inscription states *"When shall modesty and uncorrupted fidelity, the sister of justice and naked trustfulness, to thee find any equal.*

CAPTAIN W T P SHORTT
Circa 1812 - 1881

Over the centuries the City of Exeter has always attracted the serious historian and archaeologist. In 1832 Captain W T P Shortt took up residence in Exeter and undertook archaeological digs and the uncovering of historical artefacts. At this period changes were taking place that allowed access to previously covered sites. Shortt was to become one of the first field archaeologists. Over a period of time he accumulated significant material and paid for interesting finds. His enthusiasm would sometimes lead him into arguments with those seeking to remove much of the old city and he was regarded as controversial in his claims. He published details of his finds in one of the earliest books on archaeology of Exeter *Roman and other antiquities of Exeter*. Shortt went to live in Heidelberg, Germany and died in 1881. Samian Ware and coins collected by him are retained in Exeter's museum.

LLOYD PARRY OBE 1865 - 1950

Born in North Wales, Lloyd Parry attended Liverpool University obtaining degrees in art, science and law. Working in the legal department of The County Council of West Riding he came to Exeter as Town Clerk in 1905. For twenty-five years he managed the affairs of Exeter seeing the annexation of Heavitree and St Thomas for Poor Law purposes, the purchasing of Rougemont House and gardens, the start of a new library and the provision of The Civic Hall. Lloyd Parry supported the development of education and the development of the University of the South West. Undertaking service in the First World War he was awarded the OBE and Belgian Ordre de la Couronne. On retirement he became Governor of The Royal Albert Memorial Museum and The City Library and was president of the Exeter branch of NALGO. Lloyd Parry is recognised for his books on Exeter *The history of Exeter Guildhall and Life Within (1956), The history of The Royal Albert Memorial College, Exeter(1946),) Local Government (1934),Medieval council of Exeter (1931), St Nicholas Priory (1929), The founding of Exeter School (1913) and. Exeter civic seals (1909)* Town Clerk, Honorary Lecturer on Constitutional Law and public administration and a bachelor Lloyd Parry

lived at 7, Baring Place, Exeter and died at the age of 85 on December 1st 1950. The funeral service at Southernhay Congregrational Church was attended by a very large congregation including Mayors and Sheriffs, councillors, numerous dignitaries and representatives from organisations and institutions.

HENRY FREDERICK WILLEY 1830 - 1904

Henry Willey started work in Exeter for a local gas company and took over the business in 1868. It was to thrive making gas stoves, gas meters and other gas appliances. The slot gas meter was invented by Willeys of Exeter and became a substantial part of the business. The company was to employ a large number of people with nearly one thousand workers at its peak. Henry became an eminent businessman and involved with politics and in 1892 and 1893 became Mayor of Exeter. A pioneering businessman he sent a contingency of his staff to America to study conditions and new methods of production. It is said that one of the first cars in England was possibly built at Willey's. Henry Willey died in 1904, aged forty one, leaving a substantial business behind him.

REVEREND SABINE BARING GOULD 1834 - 1924

Sabine Baring Gould was born on the 28th January 1834 in an elegant period house situated at the entry to Dix's Field, Exeter and was baptised in St Sidwell's Church. As a young man he was sent to Kings College School London. The Gould family owned an estate at Lew Trenchard inherited by his father and later passed on to Sabine. He took up the task of restoring the church and manor house that had fallen into a bad state of repair. Baring Gould was particularly interested in books and writing, becoming a well known novelist on the west country,. He was to write on history and religion and he also wrote hymns, the most famous being *"Onward Christian soldiers"*. Sabine Baring Gould became Rector of Lew Trenchard from 1881 to 1924. He died at the age of 89 on January 2nd 1924 after being ill for a period of time.

EDWARD BOWRING STEPHENS 1815 - 1882

The Victorian era is famous for its love of statues, figures and works of art of which some are to be seen around the city. Edward Bowring Stephens, sculptor, was born in Exeter in 1815 and by the end of his life had left a considerable legacy. He was brilliant from a young age and worked in Rome, Naples and Exeter. In 1842 he went to live in London where he had a studio. He received numerous commissions and was awarded a gold medal by the Royal Academy in 1843. He also exhibited at The Great Exhibition in 1851. The numerous commissions included works for Devon families and the City of Exeter. This is reflected in statues seen in Northernhay Gardens that include Thomas Dyke Acland, Earl Fortescue, John Dinham and the famous bronze The Deer Stalker. A bust by him of Prince Albert is also seen in Exeter museum. He died in London aged 67 on 10th November 1882.

GENERAL REDVERS BULLER
1839 - 1908
Redvers Buller was born at a large country house called Downes at the edge of Crediton in 1839. He was to become a famous Victorian General and is best remembered as General of the South African Boer War where he relieved the famous siege of Ladysmith and was a man of courage and character. After studying at Eton College he became a great soldier and leader having an extensive career between 1859 and 1900. He was awarded the Victoria Cross. After retiring he farmed and enjoyed breeding horses and the famous Devon Red cattle. A large bronze statue was erected to General Buller at the junction of Cowley Road and Hele Road where it can still be seen today. General Buller attended the unveiling of the statue on the 6th September 1905. He died in 1908.

HARRY HEMS 1842 - 1916
Harry Hems was born in Yorkshire in 1842 and was to become one of the most famous ecclesiastical sculptors in the country. At the age of fourteen he went to work for a cutlery firm in Sheffield but disliked it and took up carving. He later spent time in Italy studying art and sculpture. Hems was contacted by Exeter Museum who required new capitals to be carved for the front of the building. On arriving at St David's Station he found a horseshoe at his feet and took this as a good omen and gained the commission for the museum. Staying in Exeter he created an extensive studio and works in Longbrook Street employing around one hundred people. His work was much sought after and one of his famous pieces was an exact replica of the Speaker's Chair from Parliament. It was exported to Canada. Harry Hems died on 5th January 1916 and was buried in the Higher Cemetery.

Castle St College Hostel.

JESSIE MONTGOMERY
1851 - 1918

Jessie Montgomery born 6th August 1851 was the daughter of Canon Cook who lived in Exeter's Cathedral Close. As a young woman Jessie became deeply involved in the expansion of education and reform. She worked tirelessly pioneering University extension lectures and supported the Workers Education Association and teacher training. In 1902 she opened a college for women student teachers at Bradninch Hall, Castle Street and acted as the Warden. In 1964 Jessie Montgomery was recognised for her work with a hall for women students being named after her at Exeter University. A marble tablet in Exeter Cathedral also commemorates her. She died in 1918.

FRED KARNO   1866 - 1941

Frederick John Westcott was born in Paul Street, Exeter on 26th March 1866. As a young man he became indentured as a

plumber but entered into circus and pantomime. He created opportunities for new stage talent and became a well known music hall comedian and later an impresario. Fred was responsible for launching the young Charlie Chaplin, Stan Laurel, Bud Flanagan, and many others on the road to fame with his vaudeville company that toured America in 1910. He adopted the name of Fred Karno for his business and returned to Exeter in 1908, opening a theatre in the London Inn Square that had previously been Assembly Rooms but was renamed The Hippodrome Theatre. It closed in 1931. Fred Karno died of diabetes at the age of seventy five in Poole, Dorset in 1941.

SIR EDWIN LANDSEER LUTYENS
1869 - 1944

Sir Edwin Landseer Lutyens was one of Britain's finest architects and was born in London and died there. This remarkable man learnt his skills from watching local builders and craftsmen. He studied at the Kensington School of Art and received his first commission at the age of twenty. Edwin formed a friendship with Gertrude Jekyll, the Victorian garden designer. Together they designed houses and gardens and left a wonderful legacy. During his lifetime Lutyens designed many famous buildings but is internationally recognised for his plan for the rebuilding of Delhi, India. He was also to design the last castle in England, Castle Drogo at Drewsteignton, Devon. He also was responsible for the design of the County War Memorial in Exeter's Cathedral Yard unveiled in 1921 by the Prince of Wales.

ETHEL LEGA-WEEKES 1864 - 1949
Historian Ethel Lega-Weekes, of noted Italian ancestry, was born in 1864 and lived with her mother in Topsham Road, Exeter where she remained until her death in 1949. Ethel was to become well known in the city for her historical research work and became a Fellow of the Royal Historical Society. She made many contributions to the Devon Notes & Queries and the Transactions of The Devonshire Association and is known for her book *"Topography of the Cathedral Close, Exeter"* printed in 1915 and other publications. Ethel Lega-Weekes championed the preservation of Polsoe Priory and often worked with Arthur Everett, historian and archaeologist.

JOHN "BABBACOMBE" LEE 1864 - 1933
In 1885 John Lee, aged 17, was convicted of killing his employer at Babbacombe in Devon. He was sentenced to be hanged at Exeter Prison but protested his innocence. The day of the execution arrived and John Lee stood on the trap with the noose around his neck. The bolt to the trap door was withdrawn but he remained standing much to the astonishment of the officials. The executioner went through the procedure again but again it failed. A last attempt was made but again it failed. Lee was taken back to his cell and after discussion with The Home Secretary John Lee was sentenced to life imprisonment. After a period of twenty two years he left prison in 1907. Lee travelled to America and in 2009 his final resting place was traced to Milwaukee USA. He became known as *"The man they couldn't hang"*

SIDNEY ENDACOTT 1885 - 1918
Born in Ashburton Sidney Endacott attended Blundells School at Tiverton but lived in Exeter. He was artistically inclined and took up a profession with J Wippell & Co Ecclesiastical and Domestic Furnishers as a sculptor and

woodcarver and worked with stained glass. His brothers left for the USA in 1893 and shortly after Sidney followed them to Lawrence, Kansas. His skills were recognised and he was commissioned to undertake carvings at a substantial villa called The Castle. After three years he returned to England and married in 1903. Sidney obtained the role of a tutor at Exeter School of Art and also became a prolific artist. His work, produced for the commercial market, was printed as black and white postcards that were hand-tinted and sold through Worth & Co in the Cathedral Close. Many of his images reflected Exeter historical buildings and events and sold as sets. Sidney Endacott died in 1918 and was buried in the Higher Cemetery where his tombstone incorporates an artist's palette.

ARTHUR EVERETT   1889 - 1979

Arthur Everett was to become a well recognised figure in Exeter. In his early years as a tram driver he was fascinated by the city's buildings and architecture and was to become a self taught archaeologist and a Fellow of The Society of Antiquaries, and joined the Vernacular Architecture Society. His knowledge became extensive and he worked on many of Exeter's earliest buildings and sites. He undertook surveys, drawings and descriptions of buildings including St Katherine's Priory, Bowhill and St Loye's Chapel. Arthur often worked in conjunction with Ethel Lega–Weekes and also contributed to The Devon Notes and Queries and the Transactions of the Devonshire Association. Arthur Everett lived in Old Tiverton Road and died at the age of 90.

HENRY WALTER SWEET
1889 - 1943

A West Country artist Henry Walter Sweet is known for his street scenes, seascapes and general views. He studied at the Exeter School of Art under the direction of his friend, artist and Headmaster of the School of Art, John Shapland. Walter worked locally and exhibited at the Devon and Exeter Annual Exhibition and at the Eland Gallery in High Street Exeter. Sweet and Shapland collaborated on a book titled simply *Exeter – sketches by W H Sweet with plan.* The twenty five page book sold for one shilling and was produced around 1927. The pencil sketches depict Exeter's old buildings, street scenes and features.

Following World War Two Sweet joined the Devonshire Regiment and was posted abroad. On his return he moved to Dundee and worked for James Valentine as an illustrator.

He died on 12th February 1943 at the age of 53.

**IRENE VANBURGH 1872 - 1949
and VIOLET VANBURGH
1867 - 1942**

Sisters, Irene and Violet Vanburgh were born at Heavitree Vicarage, the daughters of Prebendary Barnes in 1867 and 1872. Their father was opposed to corporal punishment and dealt with their offences by making them wear odd woollen socks, sometimes a black one and striped one. Irene attended a theatrical school in Margate where she specialised in comedy. She appeared at Exeter's' Theatre Royal, the last time being in 1945. The actress celebrated a Golden Jubilee Testimonial Matinee in 1938 and was made a Dame of the Empire in 1941. Her sister Violet's theatrical career ran on similar lines, first appearing in burlesque in 1886. Later she toured America with the Kendals, and on her return played Anne Boleyn in Irving's production of Henry VIII and also understudied the famous Ellen Terry. She was considered a woman of elegance and ability. A plaque commemorates both actresses in Exeter Cathedral.

JOHN SHAPLAND   1865 - 1929

Born in Dawlish on 1st December 1865, John Shapland became interested in drawing from an early age but later apprenticed to a house decorator at Thorverton. He also attended evening classes at Exeter School of Art. There is photographic evidence that John may have been involved with creating decorative plaster ceilings at Killerton House. Qualifying for his Art Masters Certificate he studied at South Kensington School of Art. He was appointed Art Master at Exeter School of Art progressing to Headmaster. On retirement he took up painting full time, travelling extensively and painting British

beauty spots. He purchased Nos 1 & 2 Catherine Street creating *The Cathedral Art Gallery* in the 1920s. His commercial work in the form of postcards, prints and calendars were known as Brunotypes and sold from the premises. His major works were exhibited in London and the provinces, the Doré Gallery Bond Street, The Royal Academy and in the United States. John Shapland had six sons and six daughters. He died at the age of 64 on 10th November 1929 and is buried in the Higher Cemetery.

F J WIDGERY 1891 - 1942

Frederick John Widgery, born in Exeter in 1861 was the son of artist William Widgery, and followed in his father's footsteps. He was to become a very well known and prolific artist and is still popular today. Educated in the Cathedral School and the Exeter School of Art he progressed to the South Kensington Museum and studied in Antwerp, returning to Exeter in 1890. Widgery started a studio in Queen Street and also became involved with local politics, becoming Mayor in 1903-1904, He was made a Freeman of Exeter in 1905 and a City Alderman in 1909. He was involved with the instigation of The Exeter Pictorial Record Society, a photo archive to record the changing city of Exeter. As an artist he became known for his studies of Dartmoor, moorland scenes, seascapes and harbours. His work was also used for illustrating books and for railway posters, helping to attract tourists to the West Country. He exhibited in London at the Royal Academy and The Walker Gallery Art Gallery, Liverpool. Frederick John Widgery died on 27th January 1942 at the age of 81.

JOHN ANGEL FRBS 1881 - 1960

The sculptor John Angel was born in Newton Abbot in 1881, the son of a tailor. The family moved to St Thomas in Exeter and John was apprenticed as a wood carver. He attended the Exeter School of Art, The Lambeth School of Art and The Academy School. John Angel stayed in London and became elected as a Fellow of the Royal Society of British Sculptors. He was commissioned in 1921 to create the Exeter War Memorial on a site previously occupied by Northernhay House in Northernhay Gardens. The memorial with five superb bronze figures is recognised as being one of the finest war memorials in the country. John Angel left England for the USA in 1928 where he became one of the most noted sculptors in the country and received many important commissions. He died in America on October 16th 1960.

HENRY WYKES 1874 - 1964

The Exeter photographer Henry Wykes was born in Grantham in April 1875, and became interested in art in his early years. At the age of thirteen he went to sea remaining until he was eighteen. He sketched scenes of Hamburg and Antwerp and produced portraits, becoming a self taught painter. He studied art at Antwerp from 1893 to 1894. Married in 1896 the family left for Australia but returned to Exeter in 1912 where Henry bought the Exe Bridge Photographic Studio. Supplying studio portraits and paintings the studio went from strength to strength. Well connected Henry moved to Bedford Circus and finally to 4 Northernhay Place from 1939. The Henry Wykes Studio attracted high society and Henry and his later partner Marjorie Hockmuth undertook portraiture, interiors, industrial and commercial work. Henry Wykes died in 1964 but Marjorie continued until 1974 and finally closed the studio. At this time the negative stock was 42,000 images. The entire negative stock was saved by photographer Peter Thomas who created The Isca Historical Photographic Collection in 1974.

THOMAS SHARP 1901 - 1978

In 1943 the Town Planner and writer Thomas Sharp was employed by the Exeter City Council to produce plans for the rebuilding of Exeter after the devastation of May 4th 1942. Approximately one third of the city had been destroyed. Thomas Sharp was the Senior Research officer for the Ministry of Town and County Planning. In 1945 Thomas Sharp prepared an exhibition that was held at the City Library for two weeks. His controversial plans for the city attracted thousands of people between 29th December and 19th January 1946. His ideas for Exeter included one of the first pedestrian precincts in the country that was to have one of the finest views of an English cathedral; however many of his other proposals were not instigated. The project was produced as a book and called *The Exeter Phoenix* and published for the City Council in 1946. Thomas Sharp is recognised as being one of the key figures in English Town Planning in the twentieth century and was the author of one of the foremost books on town planning.

Dr W G HOSKINS 1908 - 1992

William George Hoskins, the son of a baker, was born in St David's Hill, Exeter on May 22nd 1908. He attended Hele's School and the University College of the South West and was to become Lecturer at University College Leicester, founding the first University Department of Local History. In 1952 he was to leave Leicester taking up a post as a Reader in Economic History at the University of Oxford. Retaining his links with Exeter he was one of the founders of The Exeter Civic Society in 1960 and President of the Dartmoor Preservation Association from 1962-1976. In 1960 his well known book *Two thousand years in Exeter* was published. In 1976 he gained national recognition for the BBC series *The landscape of England*. Dr Hoskins produced twenty publications including *Devon and its People, Trade and People in Exeter 1688-1800* and *Devon* (reprinted 1992). He was awarded the Fellowship of the British Academy in 1969 and also a CBE before 1974. The University of Exeter bestowed a Doctorate of Letters on him in 1974. He died on January 11th 1992.

HERBERT READ 1908 - 1950

Herbert Read senior held a position with the well known Exeter ecclesiastical sculptors of Harry Hems in Longbrook Street and became a chief designer for the company. In 1888 he set up his own works in Sidwell Street *The St Sidwell Artworks*. The company sometimes worked with Harry Hems but had specialised more in restoration. In 1908 Herbert Read junior took over from his father and ran the company until 1950. Ecclesiastical woodcarving was a speciality and the company obtained numerous prestigious projects. Herbert Read was employed by Exeter Cathedral and following immense damage in May 1942 Herbert Read undertook a remarkable restoration of a medieval wooden Cathedral screen that had been shattered into hundreds of pieces. Gathering all the fragments he could find Herbert Read completely reconstructed the medieval screen - an extraordinary feat - and left a remarkable legacy to the Cathedral that can still be seen today.

JACQUELINE WARREN
1912- 1991

French-born Jacqueline Warren was educated in Paris and spent time in England and Spain studying languages. She met her Husband, Bob Warren, in London and later they moved to Exeter where she became interested in its history and buildings but had first become attracted to architecture, buildings and townscapes whilst on visits to Italian cities. As a freelance writer she contributed articles to national newspapers, magazines and professional journals. A long relationship developed with Exeter's Express & Echo newspaper which featured her articles for many years. She was appointed Curator of St Nicholas Priory by The City Council in 1959 until 1973. In the late 1970s she was approached by local author and historian Peter Thomas with a view to collaborating on a major Exeter book. *Aspects of Exeter,* first published in 1980, was to be the culmination of her work, becoming a best seller, and later recognised as an academic study of Exeter. It was reprinted in 2006. Jacqueline Warren died in 1991.

LADY AILEEN FOX 1907- 2005

The pioneering archaeologist Aileen Mary Fox was born on 29th July 1907 and educated in Kent and she read English at Newnham College Cambridge. She volunteered for excavations in Richborough and went on to excavate sites across the UK with her husband. She obtained her title after her husband was knighted. In 1945 she was offered the opportunity to excavate Exeter after the devastation of the war. It provided remarkable opportunities as much of the city had been laid bare due to bomb damage and demolition.

Her work was assisted by the use of six Italian prisoners of war. Aileen Fox published her findings in the book *Roman Exeter* published in 1952. In 1955 she became Special Lecturer in Archaeology at the University of the South West and Senior Lecturer from 1947 -1972. After retiring from the University in 1972 she spent ten years in New Zealand also undertaking archaeology.

Lady Aileen Fox is recognised as the founder of modern archaeology in the South West of England She died in Exeter on 21st November 2005.